SandCastle 2

More Blends

ng

Carey Molter

ABDO
Publishing Company

Published by SandCastle™, an imprint of ABDO Publishing Company, 4940 Viking Drive, Edina, Minnesota 55435.

Printed in the United States.

Cover and interior photo credits: Artville, Eyewire Images, PhotoDisc, Rubberball Productions.

Library of Congress Cataloging-in-Publication Data

Molter, Carey, 1973-
    Ng / Carey Molter.
       p. cm. -- (Blends)
    ISBN 1-57765-450-1
     1. Readers (Primary) [1. Readers.] I. Title. II. Blends (Series)

PE1119 .M625 2001
428.1--dc21

00-056564

The SandCastle concept, content, and reading method have been reviewed and approved by a national advisory board including literacy specialists, librarians, elementary school teachers, early childhood education professionals, and parents.

## Let Us Know

After reading the book, SandCastle would like you to tell us your stories about reading. What is your favorite page? Was there something hard that you needed help with? Share the ups and downs of learning to read. We want to hear from you! To get posted on the ABDO Publishing Company Web site, send us email at:

**sandcastle@abdopub.com**

# About SandCastle™
## Nonfiction books for the beginning reader

- Basic concepts of phonics are incorporated with integrated language methods of reading instruction. Most words are short, and phrases, letter sounds, and word sounds are repeated.

- Readability is determined by the number of words in each sentence, the number of characters in each word, and word lists based on curriculum frameworks.

- Full-color photography reinforces word meanings and concepts.

- "Words I Can Read" list at the end of each book teaches basic elements of grammar, helps the reader recognize the words in the text, and builds vocabulary.

- Reading levels are indicated by the number of flags on the castle.

## Look for more SandCastle books in these three reading levels:

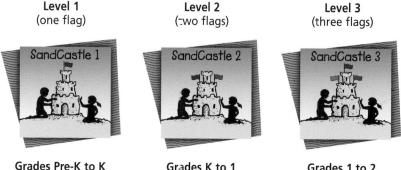

| Level 1<br>(one flag) | Level 2<br>(two flags) | Level 3<br>(three flags) |
|:---:|:---:|:---:|
| **Grades Pre-K to K**<br>5 or fewer words per page | **Grades K to 1**<br>5 to 10 words per page | **Grades 1 to 2**<br>10 to 15 words per page |

We are young.

We do something fun
every day.

Angus sticks out his
tongue.

He does not like
kisses.

7

**ng**

Channing likes to eat toast first thing in the morning.

**ng**

Inga loves her long braids.

She does not have bangs.

Ingrid and her friend
hang together on the
bar.

13

Irving feels strong
when he swings and
hits the ball.

15

**ng**

This butterfly clings to her hand.

Its wings are pretty.

**ng**

These boys use their lungs to sing a loud song.

**ng**

What does Sterling
wear on her ears?

(earrings)

# Words I Can Read

## Nouns

### A noun is a person, place, or thing

ball (BAWL) p. 15
bar (BAR) p. 13
butterfly (BUHT-ur-flye)
  p. 17
day (DAY) p. 5
friend (FREND) p. 13

hand (HAND) p. 17
morning (MOR-ning) p. 9
song (SAWNG) p. 19
thing (THING) p. 9
toast (TOAST) p. 9
tongue (TUHNG) p. 7

## Plural Nouns

### A plural noun is more than one person, place, or thing

bangs (BANGZ) p. 11
braids (BRAYDZ) p. 11
boys (BOYZ) p. 19
ears (IHRZ) p. 21

earrings (IHR-ingz) p. 21
kisses (KISS-ez) p. 7
lungs (LUHNGZ) p. 19
wings (WINGZ) p. 17

## Proper Nouns

### A proper noun is the name of a person, place, or thing

Angus (ANG-uhs) p. 7
Channing (CHAN-ing) p. 9
Inga (ING-uh) p. 11

Ingrid (ING-rid) p. 13
Irving (IRV-ing) p. 15
Sterling (STER-ling) p. 21

**22**

# Verbs

**A verb is an action or being word**

**are** (AR) pp. 5, 17
**clings** (KLINGZ) p. 17
**do** (DOO) p. 5
**does** (DUHZ) pp. 7, 11, 21
**eat** (EET) p. 9
**feels** (FEELZ) p. 15
**hang** (HANG) p. 13
**have** (HAV) p. 11
**hits** (HITSS) p. 15

**like** (LIKE) p. 7
**likes** (LIKESS) p. 9
**loves** (LUVZ) p. 11
**sing** (SING) p. 19
**sticks** (STIKSS) p. 7
**swings** (SWINGZ) p. 15
**use** (YOOZ) p. 19
**wear** (WAIR) p. 21

# Adjectives

**An adjective describes something**

**every** (EV-ree) p. 5
**first** (FURST) p. 9
**fun** (FUHN) p. 5
**her** (HUR) pp. 11, 13, 17, 21
**his** (HIZ) p. 7
**its** (ITS) p. 17
**long** (LAWNG) p. 11

**loud** (LOUD) p. 19
**pretty** (PRIT-ee) p. 17
**strong** (STRONG) p. 15
**their** (THAIR) p. 19
**these** (THEEZ) p. 19
**this** (THISS) p. 17
**young** (YUHNG) p. 5

# Match these ng Words
## to the Pictures

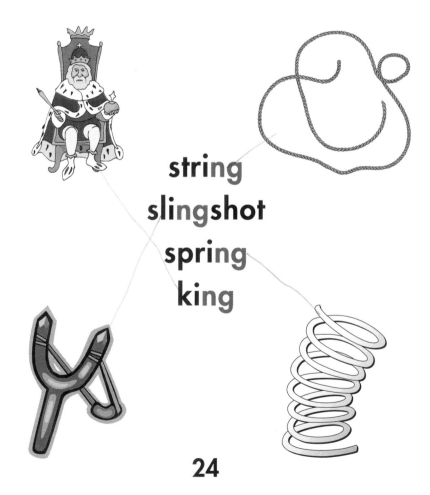

string

slingshot

spring

king